SQUADRONS!

No. 37

THE SUPERMARINE

SPITFIRE MK. XIV
- THE BELGIAN & DUTCH SQUADRONS -

PHIL H. LISTEMANN

ISBN: 979-1096490-58-5

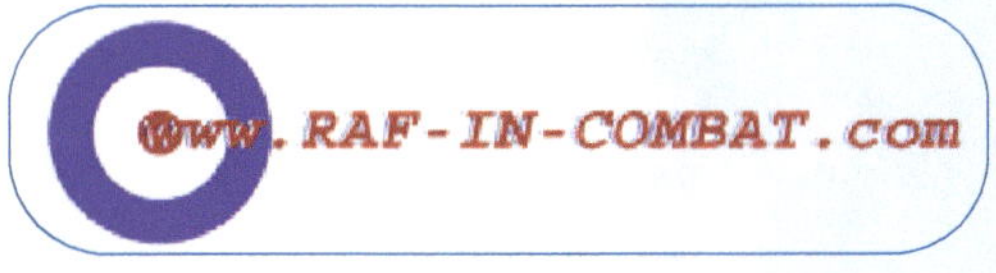

Colour profiles: Gaetan Marie/Bravo Bravo Aviation

PERSONEL :
(AUS)/RAF: Australian serving in the RAF
(BEL)/RAF: Belgian serving in the RAF
(CAN)/RAF: Canadian serving in the RAF
(CZ)/RAF: Czechoslovak serving in the RAF
(NFL)/RAF: Newfoundlander serving in the RAF
(NL)/RAF: Dutch serving in the RAF
(NZ)/RAF: New Zealander serving in the RAF
(POL)/RAF: Pole serving in the RAF
(RHO)/RAF: Rhodesian serving in the RAF
(SA)/RAF: South African serving in the RAF
(US)/RAF - RCAF : American serving in the RAF or RCAF

RANKS
G/C : Group Captain
W/C : Wing Commander
S/L : Squadron Leader
F/L : Flight Lieutenant
F/O : Flying Officer
P/O : Pilot Officer
W/O : Warrant Officer
F/Sgt : Flight Sergeant
Sgt : Sergeant
Cpl : Corporal
LAC : Leading Aircraftman

OTHER
ATA: Air Transport Auxiliary
CO : Commander
DFC : Distinguished Flying Cross
DFM : Distinguished Flying Medal
DSO : Distinguished Service Order
Eva. : Evaded
ORB : Operational Record Book
OTU : Operational Training Unit
PoW : Prisoner of War
PAF: Polish Air Force
RAF : Royal Air Force
RAAF : Royal Australian Air Force
RCAF : Royal Canadian Air Force
RNZAF : Royal New Zealand Air Force
SAAF : South African Air Force
s/d: Shot down
Sqn : Squadron
† : Killed

CODENAMES - OFFENSIVE OPERATIONS - FIGHTER COMMAND

CIRCUS:
Bombers heavily escorted by fighters, the purpose being to bring enemy fighters into combat.

RAMROD:
Bombers escorted by fighters, the primary aim being to destroy a target.

RANGER:
Large formation freelance intrusion over enemy territory with aim of wearing down enemy fighters.

RHUBARB:
Freelance fighter sortie against targets of opportunity.

ROADSTEAD:
Dive bombing and low level attacks on enemy ships at sea or in harbour

RODEO:
A fighter sweep without bombers.

SWEEP:
An offensive flight by fighters designed to draw up and clear the enemy from the sky.

THE SUPERMARINE SPITFIRE MK. XIV

The first Griffon-powered Spitfires suffered from poor high altitude performance due to only having a single stage supercharger. Therefore, the first operational variant, the Mk.XII, was primarily used for operations at low altitude (see SQUADRONS! 5), but the combination was very promising. By 1943, Rolls-Royce engineers had developed a new Griffon engine, the 61 series, with a two-stage supercharger. In the end a slightly modified engine, the 65 series, was used in the Mk.XIV. The resulting aircraft provided a substantial performance increase over the Merlin-powered Mk.IX and performed well at all altitudes. Although initially based on the Mk.VIII airframe, continuous improvements saw later aircraft sporting a cut-down rear fuselage, tear-drop canopies, and the E-Type wing with heavier armament.

The Mk.XIV differed from the Mk.XII in that the longer, two-stage supercharged Griffon 65, producing 2050 hp (1528 kW), was mounted 10 inches (25.4 cm) further forward. A new five-bladed Rotol propeller was used and was the most obvious visual difference compared to earlier marks. The increased cooling requirements of the Griffon meant all radiators were considerably larger and the underwing housings were deeper than previous versions. The Mk.XIV also had a bigger oil tank and other improvements were made. The first batch of aircraft to fly with the Griffon 60 series engines were six converted Mk.VIIIs (JF316 to JF321). The first one of these was flown on 20 January 1943, with production ordered following a series of trials. The first aircraft left the production line in October 1943 following the amendment of existing Spitfire contracts. The XIV was initially seen as an interim design pending the Spitfire Mk.XVIII's availability. Delays with the XVIII meant the XIV became one of the major Spitfire fighter variants and a valuable asset for the RAF during the final year of the war. The design was also improved by the end of the war, as mentioned above, with tear-drop canopy aircraft, equipped with two 0.50-in machine guns (and the standard pair of cannons) in place of the four ubiquitous, but obsolete, 0.303-in weapons, beginning to reach operational units in 1945. This later variant was known as the Mk.XIVE. The XIV was built as a fighter, but was also developed for fighter-reconnaissance (FR) to replace the effective, but ageing, Mustang in the Tac/R role. In total, 957 Mk.XIVs were built, more than 430 of which were FR Mk.XIVs, the last being taken on charge by the RAF in October 1945. Examples had already begun to reach the Far East when the war ended in August 1945. The mark remained in service with the RAF and various foreign air forces, including Belgium, well after the war.

List of serials:

RB142 is typical of the first Spitfire XIVs with its classic canopy and four 0-303-in machine guns. This aircraft was lost in July 1944 while serving with 610 Sqn, the first RAF unit to be equipped with the type.

MV259 was built as a fighter-reconnaissance aircraft (FR.XIV) and was issued to the Canadian 414 Squadron shortly after VE-Day.

Of an order placed on 27 July 142 for 700 Spitfires, 75 were actually built as Mk.XIVs – **MT847-858, MV246-MV273, MV286-MV320,** and **MV347-MV386** – and were delivered between February and April 1945.

From the third order placed on 1 December 1942 for 225 Spitfires, 192 were built as Mk.XIVs – **NH637-NH661, NH685-NH720, NH741-NH759, NH775-NH813, NH831-NH846, NH857-NH875,** and **NH892-NH929** – and were delivered between November 1944 and June 1945.

From the fourth order placed on 29 December 1942, but later cancelled and partially reinstated, ten Mk.XIVs were delivered in March and April 1945 – **NM814-NM823.** Fifty-seven were cancelled.

From the eighth order, placed on 14 August 1943, fifty Mk.XIVs were delivered between December 1943 and March 1944 – **RB140-RB189.**

From the tenth order placed on 23 October 1943 for 406 Mk.XIVs and XIXs. In all, 384 were delivered between April 1944 and May 1945 – **RM615-RM625, RM648-RM656, RM670-RM713, RM726-RM770, RM783-RM825, RM839-RM887, RM901-RM943, RM957-RM999, RN113-RN160,** and **RN172-RN221.**

From the eleventh order placed on 12 February 1944 for 150 Spitfire Mk.IXs, 79 were built as Mk.XIVs and delivered between February 1945 and August 1945 – **SM812-SM842, SM876-SM899,** and **SM913-SM938.**

An order placed in August 1944 for Spitfire F.21s saw six delivered as Mk.XIVs in May 1945 – **TP236-TP240,** and **TP256.** TP236 was retained by Vickers-Armstrong, but was eventually handed over in November 1945.

The order placed on 23 February 1945, for 157 Spitfires, ultimately included 120 Mk.XIVs – **TX974-TX998, TZ102-TZ149, TZ152-TZ176,** and **TZ178-TZ199.** The deliveries took place between May and October 1945.

The Spitfire XIV was initially deployed in Great Britain with ADGB and participated in the V-1 interception campaign. By the summer of 1944, the number of squadrons remained limited to three (91, 322, 610), but, with more airframes becoming available, it was decided to send the Spitfire XIV to the Continent to serve with 2 TAF, as replacements for the Mustang Mk.III, from September 1944. It was with 2 TAF that the Mk.XIV would prove it was far more than just an interceptor. The number of squadrons was increased to four (41, 130, 350, 402), plus two in the tactical reconnaissance role, Nos. 2 and 430, but this included a turnover of squadrons with the first three units being re-equipped with older types as they stayed at home. The number of Mk.XIVs available was still not enough to equip squadrons earmarked to stay in the UK. Other squadrons were converted during the final days of the war in Europe when production reached its peak, but they saw limited action, if any while other airframes began to reach the Far East. The type enjoyed a long post-war career with the last operational units flying it until the beginning of the fifties and surplus machines largely exported wherever possible. During the war, only two squadrons manned by non-Commonwealth pilots flew the XIV, the Belgian 350 and the Dutch 322, but they were not equipped with the aircraft at the same time. Their operational usage is described below.

The Belgians flew with J.E. Johnson, the RAF's official top-scorer of WW2, twice when 350 Sqn was part of 125 and 127 Wings of 2TAF. After several attempts, Johnson was finally accepted into the RAF in August 1939. Completing his training, he was first posted to 19 Sqn in August 1940 before moving to 616 (South Yorkshire) Squadron the following month. He made his first claim on 15 January 1941, sharing a Do17 damaged. By the end of September his tally had increased steadily, including a double claim on 21 September, and he was awarded the DFC that month. By that time he was acting as a flight commander. In June 1942 a Bar was added to his DFC. The next month he left the squadron to take command of 610 (County of Chester) Squadron. He remained in this position until March 1943 when he left to lead the Kenley Wing. On 15 June, he made a second double claim over Fw190s and the same month was awarded the DSO. A Bar followed in September before he was rested for the next six months. In March 1944 he returned to operations and, posted as wing leader, led 144 (RCAF) Wing during the Normandy landings. He had claimed another ten victories by July, including three double claims (5 April, 28 June and 5 July). When the Wing was disbanded in mid-July, he became WingCo Flying of 127 (RCAF) Wing, earning a second Bar to his DSO in the meantime, and added another double claim on 23 August. He made his last claim with this unit on 27 September, a Bf109 destroyed, to bring his total to 41 confirmed victories (seven shared), five probables (two shared) and thirteen damaged (three shared). He led the Wing until March 1945 when he was promoted to group captain and was appointed OC of 125 Wing until the end of the war. He remained with the RAF after the war and retired as an Air Vice-Marshal in March 1966.

THE BELGIANS AND THE DUTCH IN THE RAF

Belgium and The Netherlands entered the war in May 1940 when they were invaded by Germany. Dutch resistance ended after five days and eighteen for the Belgians. By late May 1940, the Belgians had 180 pilots and ground crew in Britain who had escaped from Belgium or France. They wanted them gathered into a Belgian unit, like the Dutch did early in June, but that request was initially denied by the British because a large injection of RAF technical personnel would have been required to make the units operational. The Belgians were quickly re-trained and sent individually to various RAF combat units. About thirty of them participated in the Battle of Britain. This arrangement remained until the middle of 1941 when it was accepted that the Belgians could have their own units. It started slowly, however, with the formation of one flight into No. 131 (County of Kent) Squadron at the end of June 1941. This flight would serve as the nucleus for No. 350 (Belgian) Squadron at the end of the year. By that time the number of Belgians was enough to man a squadron without the support of RAF technical personnel. This time taken to form the squadron can be explained by the fact that the Belgians were almost entirely dependent on escapees from Europe, rather than volunteers from elsewhere, to build up their own force. However, they also had another asset to offer the British, their huge African colony, the Belgian Congo. Early in 1942, the Belgian authorities were extremely anxious about the vulnerability of the colony. To reinforce its defences, it was decided to raise two squadrons, one patrol unit with long-range aircraft to provide protection to the convoys, and one fighter squadron, although the need for the latter unit in the colony was less pressing. For the British, however, the threat was not that big, but it was finally agreed material would be provided to form a new fighter squadron, No. 349, with available Belgian personnel and British technical bods, the latter only temporarily. After much discussion among the politicians, 349 would, in the end, be based in West Africa, where the British needed a fighter presence that could be deployed to North Africa if required, and not in the Congo. Numbers 349 and 350 Squadrons were the only Belgian fighter units in the RAF during WW2.

For the Dutch, the situation was slightly different. While they were able to form their first squadrons as early as June 1940 (Nos. 320 and 321), it must be recalled that this could only be achieved because they had spirited away material and personnel, in this case Dutch Navy personnel, from under the noses of the Germans. The Dutch Army had its own service and many of its personnel had found asylum in Britain, but, from the start, the number of trained pilots was low as The Netherlands, in May 1940, only had a small active air force. At first the British thought they would be more useful to the Dutch colonies in the East Indies where they were already operating a rather important air force, the NEIAF. However, the Dutch government in exile notified the British that new arrivals would remain to fight against the Germans. Politics slowed the process of integration in many ways, the Dutch being split between the will to fight the Germans (while the RAF needed any pilot it could get) and the need to reinforce the East Indies against the increasing Japanese threat. For the Dutch personnel in the UK who had family in Holland, the decision to be incorporated into the NEIAF was not an automatic one and they were largely reluctant to do so. In any case, the Dutch pilots had to be trained or re-trained and, when available, posted to existing RAF squadrons. There were not enough to form a full Dutch fighter unit, and no clear decision was made in 1941, so the situation remained unresolved until Java surrendered to the Japanese in March 1942. From then, the solution was simple. Some additional Dutch personnel were repatriated to Britain after that date, but they had nowhere else to go. It opened the door to the formation of a full Dutch fighter squadron. A specific Dutch unit, as with the Belgians, saw its birth as a flight within an operational unit, No. 167 (Gold Coast) Squadron, which progressively formed throughout 1942. In June 1943, a Dutch fighter squadron in the RAF was finally formed. It would be the only one.

Victories - confirmed or probable claims: 33.0 + 6 V-1s

Number of sorties: *ca.* 2,300

First operational sortie:
10.08.44

Total aircraft written-off: 24

Last operational sortie:
05.05.45

Aircraft lost on operations: 20
Aircraft lost in accidents: 4

Squadron code letters:
MN

COMMANDING OFFICERS

S/L Michel Donnet	RAF No. 102522	(BEL)/RAF	...	23.10.44
S/L Léopold C. Collignon *(Inj.)*	RAF No. 116288	(BEL)/RAF	23.10.44	24.12.44
S/L Terence Spencer *(Eva.)*	RAF No. 47269	RAF	04.01.45	26.02.45
S/L Frank F. Woolley	RAF No. 105174	RAF	27.02.45	12.04.45
S/L Terence Spencer *(PoW)*	RAF No. 47269	RAF	12.04.45	19.04.45
S/L Harold E. Walmsley	RAF No. 139425	RAF	23.04.45	19.08.45
S/L Rémi Van Lierde	RAF No. 106250	(BEL)/RAF	19.08.45	...

SQUADRON USAGE

When this unit started its conversion to the Mk.XIV, it was its fourth Spitfire mark since the squadron was raised in November 1941. Led by S/L M.G.L. Donnet, 350 was still part of ADGB and was based at Westhampnett when it received orders on 8 August to move to Hawkinge for the conversion. It was a remarkably quick process with the first operational patrols carried out on the afternoon of the 10th. At that time, the Spitfire XIVs allocated to 350 were: NH661/R, NH692, NH695, NH696/J, NH711, NH718, RM655/X, RM675/W, RM693/S, RM696, RM700/B, RM701/O, RM732, RM740, RM741/F, RM748/Z, RM750/P, RM753/N, RM754/G, RM756/Y, and RM760/E, but others were taken on charge in the days that followed. There was no change to the task assigned –

When 350 Sqn received its first Spitfire XIV, the squadron was under the command of 'Mike' Donnet. He enlisted in the pre-war Belgian military forces to become a pilot. In May 1940, he was flying the Renard R.31, a Belgian co-operation aircraft, with the Army. He was made a PoW on 28 May and sent to Germany, but was released in January 1941. He returned to Belgium, but fled to Great Britain in July in a SV-4 biplane that had been hidden on the property of one of his friends. Upon arrival in England, he enlisted in the RAF, was re-trained and, in September 1941, joined 64 Sqn. In September 1942 he became a flight commander and then, eventually, the OC in March 1943. He had been awarded the DFC the previous January. His first tour ended in November. Donnet returned to operations in March 1944 as OC of 350 (Belgian) Squadron and led the unit until October when he became the WingCo Flying of the Hornchurch Wing. He led the Mustang-equipped Bentwaters Wing in the same role from February 1945. Donnet, therefore, became one the very few Belgian pilots to fly Mustangs operationally during the war. He left the Wing in August and was discharged from the RAF in October 1946. Continuing his career in the new Belgian Air Force, he reached the rank of Lieutenant-General and retired in 1975. *(A. Bar)*

RM693/MN-S, one of the first Spitfire XIVs issued to 350 Sqn, was flown by various pilots, including S/L Donnet. This aircraft participated in the first sorties carried out. It later served with Nos. 130 and 41 Squadrons during the war. *(André Bar)*

the hunt for V-1s. The first success was recorded on 15 August when F/O R. Vanderveken and Sgt H.A. Boels shared in the destruction of a V-1 in the Ashford area early that morning. The next day, two more V-1s were shot down, one in the morning and the second late in the evening (the latter being shared between two Belgian pilots). On 19 August, 350 was sent on a Ranger over occupied Belgium in the Brussels/Saint-Trond/Chievre area. The take off was set early in the morning. Reaching Etterbeck, on the outskirts of Brussels, at zero feet, F/L A. Plisnier sighted a Ju88 (reported as a Ju188) about one mile away at 11 o'clock. He turned toward the Junkers and fired a short burst at about 60° and 600 yards. The Ju88 sighted him and a good dogfight started. Plisnier understood that, owing to his speed (about 300 mph), he could not turn inside the Junkers so he climbed to 3000 feet, made a long 15° astern attack, and fired a number of successive bursts, all from less than 150 yards and closing sometimes to 75 yards. He saw strikes on the inner wings and two yellow flashes behind the cockpit. Plisnier encountered rather accurate flak, but the dogfight continued at zero feet, sometimes between trees and chimneys. Finally he broke away thinking he had run out of ammunition. He then saw the enemy aircraft put its flaps down and enter a right hand turn. Plisnier came alongside, waggled his wings twice and peeled off. The Ju88 was trying to land in a small field, but, when flying over a hedge, the right wing dropped and the aircraft crashed. The day was a very successful one as, late in the day, while the squadron continued its anti-Diver patrols, one V-1 in the morning, and another in the afternoon, were added to the scoreboard. These were followed by a claim by F/Sgt P. Leva who tipped the V-1 with his right wing, causing it to crash and explode. The Spitfire returned safely to base albeit with a bent wingtip. This was the last V-1 claimed by 350 before it switched to escort duties from the 25th. That day, the Belgians flew two Ramrods, No. 1227 in the morning and No. 1230 in the afternoon, both having Amiens as the target. The operations were uneventful as were the next ones flown, a fighter sweep, a Ranger, but a mass Rhubarb saw two locos and eight lorries destroyed The next day Spitfire RM751 was destroyed when it caught fire during start up, but the pilot, F/Sgt J. Laloux, managed to evacuate his aircraft safely. The Spitfire was eventually struck off charge on 30 September after an investigation. The rest of August was quiet, but since the conversion 350 had flown close to 500 sorties on its new aircraft.

September started intensively with 24 sorties flown on the 1st. An escort of Lancasters to the south of Lille became a mass Rhubarb during which a car and two locos were destroyed. In the afternoon another mass Rhubarb was carried with similar success: a staff car, two lorries, two flamers and two eight-wheel trucks were destroyed. At base, a V-1 hit by flak fell outside a dispersal bay and damaged three aircraft. One, RM695, was never repaired and struck off charge. Ops continued over the few next days without major incident. On the 5th, the squadron flew over the Belgian capital. The CO dropped a Belgian flag signed by all the pilots of 350. Between 7 and 9 September the weather was so bad that no flying was performed. Operations resumed on the 10th with an anti-Big Ben (the codename for hunting V-2 launch sites) op around Rotterdam. The rest of the month was spent on bomber escorts, armed recces or further Big Ben sorties. In all the squadron flew about 300 sorties in September, the last days being flown from Lympne where 130 and 350 Squadron exchanged their Spitfire XIVs, 130 joining 2 TAF on the Continent. The trade was a bad one for the

Belgians as 130 Squadron's aircraft were found to be less well maintained. Operations from Lympne started on 2 October with a Ramrod escorting Mitchells to Arnhem, but over the next two days the weather deteriorated and prevented operational flying. On the 5th, the pilots were notified (the unit had been rife with rumours beforehand) that 350 was assigned to 2 TAF on the Continent. In the meantime operations from Lympne continued with Ramrods on the 6th, 7th, 14th and 25th (the days between being hampered by bad weather and a change of command on the 23rd with F/L L. Collignon taking over). All ops were completed without major incident except the last one as five Spitfires were posted missing on return. For various reasons the five missing Spitfires landed on the Continent, Flight Lieutenant A. Plisnier and P/O P. Paco made a safe landing at Brussels, F/Sgt E. Pauwels at Grimbergen (B.60), and F/Sgt M. Morel at Anvers-Durne (B.70) while F/Sgt L. Lambrechts had to belly land in a field short of petrol, wrecking his Spitfire in the process. All were back with the squadron before the month was done. Morel, being the last to re-join on the 31st, was therefore unable to participate in the last ops of the month. These were two bomber escorts on the 28th and another on the 30th. Owing to bad weather, which prevailed for most of October, 350 did not achieve a good operational record, with only about ninety sorties flown, but November was worse with 75 sorties flown across the eight days when the weather eased. In November, the squadron recorded two operational losses, the first on the 4th when, during an escort for Lancasters, the new CO was unable to switch to his main tank (from his belly tank). That obliged him to make a forced landing in an open field in Belgium. He was safe, but the aircraft was only good for scrap. He was back at the squadron the next day. The second loss occurred on the 14th. Flying Officer F. Verpoorten and F/Sgt L. Lambrechts took off that day, for an escort to Juvincourt, and landed at Amiens (B.48). Verpoorten missed his landing and collided with barracks at the end of the runway. This was the last flight of RM671, but Verpoorten was safe. To these two losses must be added the death of F/Sgt M. Morel on the 11th during a training flight. November was a black month for the Belgians with few operations flown to compensate. Only one op was carried from Lympne, a Ramrod to Bonheim on the 3rd, but the squadron was obliged to land at Evere (B.56) on the return journey because of the bad weather. While not ideal, this proved fortuitous as the squadron was planning to move there within days. Therefore, from that date, 350 operated from Evere. The squadron was placed under 127 Wing's authority and led by W/C 'Johnnie' Johnson. No operation was flown before the 8th because of the weather, but 350 flew various patrols, the last taking off at 15.00. No one returned from this patrol. Flight Lieutenant G. Seydel and F/O R. Duchâteau landed at B.67 (Ursel), while P/O M. Doncq and F/Sgt R. Jaminé crashed, short

Pilots of 350 Sqn gathered around their new mount in August 1944:
Left to right: Flying Officers J. Brosteaux, J. Wustefeld, P. Pacco, R. Vanderveken, and J. Vanderperren (†25.12.44), F/Sgt R. Méhuys, Sgt L. Lambrechts, S/L M. Donnet (CO), F/Sgt J. Laloux, F/L J. Lavigne (B Flight CO), Flying Officers A. Van Wersch and R. Duchâteau, P/O R. Bladt and F/O P. Delorme.
On the wing: Sergeants G. Gigot and M. Doncq. On the engine: Sgt R. Huens (†23.01.45), F/Sgt M. Morel (†11.11.44), F/O R. Muls and Sgt H. Boels. On the right wing: Sgt A. Kicq, F/O P. Siroux, F/L H. Smets (supernumerary), F/L R. Hoornaert (supernumerary) and F/O A. Claesen, the latter was visiting his former unit (he was instructing at 53 OTU at the time). Some pilots, like the A Flight CO, F/L A. Plisnier, were not present that day.
(André Bar)

A line-up of 350 Squadron's Spitfire XIVs at dispersal at Hawkinge with RM748/MN-Z clearly visible. *(André Bar)*

Flying Officer J. Wustefeld standing on the wing of a Spitfire XIV. Wustefeld fled Belgium in June 1940 and was initially incorporated into the Belgian Army in England before being transferred to the RAF in September 1941. He survived the war and returned to civilian life after the war. Behind is a line-up of the unit's Spitfire XIVs with RB169/MN-F in the foreground. *(André Bar)*

of petrol, in an open field near Maldegem. Jamine's aircraft was so badly damaged that no repairs were undertaken. Over the following days, 350 flew patrols and some fighter sweeps during which the Belgians were introduced to American anti-aircraft batteries which fired at the Belgians during a fighter patrol near Aachen. Two aircraft were damaged, but they and their pilots (F/Os R. Muls and A. Van Eeckhoudt) were able to return to base without further problems. Later in the day, F/L R. Hoornaert experienced an engine failure obliging him to make a forced landing just on the Allied side of the front. He was rescued by the Americans and was back at the squadron before the end of the day. Less than a week later, the CO, while on patrol over the Houffalize-Malmedy area, was hit by flak after making a pass at a flak position. He managed to return over Allied-held territory before he baled out at low altitude, breaking his leg badly. He would be evacuated to a Hospital in England on 25 December 1944 and saw no further operational actions during the War. Two other Spitfires were also damaged that day, but less seriously. The next day an armed recce was flown over the Malmedy-St-Vith area. A column of lorries was strafed, but unfortunately the aircraft flown by F/O J. Vanderperren was hit by debris from an exploding lorry (probably full of ammunition) and was seen to crash in flames. During the attack the Belgians claimed seven lorries destroyed. On 31 December 350 made another move, this time to Y.32 (Ash-Ophoven). The new base was among the Operation *Bodenplatte* targets on 1 January 1945 when the Luftwaffe sent fighters to attack Allied bases to try to regain an advantage. One of the squadron's Spitfires was destroyed and another damaged on the ground. This attack did not disrupt the Allies that much and they were able to continue to carry out operations from that day even though many aircraft were temporarily unserviceable (350 Squadron was not totally operational). The weather actually had more of an effect on operations. On 4 January a new CO, S/L T. Spencer, arrived to assume command. He was formerly a flight commander with 41 Squadron. Meanwhile, as the number of aircraft to be repaired was so high within 2 TAF, a clever solution to make up losses was to send pilots to the UK to collect replacements. Eleven were sent to Tangmere, but they had to wait for the weather to improve to return to the Continent. There was no let up until the 12th. Little in the way of operational activity was carried out by the remaining pilots, but it must be said the weather did not help. On 14 January S/L Spencer led the Belgians for the first time, participating in a fighter sweep around St-Vith where a large concentration of vehicles was shot up. The squadron claimed the highest score of the Wing. Two days later an armed reconnaissance was led by the wing leader, the Canadian W/C G.C. Keefer. This operation was not as successful as the previous one as the squadron flew into walls of flak and F/L H. Smets' Spitfire hit badly enough to force him to bale out into captivity. No operations were flown until the 22nd because the runway was flooded. On the 22nd, the squadron provided two patrols of two aircraft each for the entire day over Bese Weert and Nygemen Volkel . That day each pilot flew twice, some of them three times. The following day, armed recces were carried out all day long and while various targets of opportunity were strafed, flak was

10

again accurate, shooting down and killing F/Sgt R. Huens. Flying low, he didn't have time to evacuate his aircraft. Armed recces continued until the end of the month, increasing the scoreboard with lorries, locos and other ground targets destroyed, without any loss to record. The squadron moved to B.78/Eindhoven on 27 January, its new home for the next two months. In February, the number of sorties more than doubled, 290 performed in all. The main task remained armed recces or patrols, as far as weather permitted, and the Belgians found many opportunities to strafe targets on the ground, but flak took its toll when F/Sgt J. Laloux was shot down around Osnabrück on the 11th and was captured. On 21 February, the Belgians escorted bombers targeting Weese. That was followed by an uneventful fighter sweep over the Rhine. That was not the case for the next one late in the afternoon. The squadron met a formation of twenty enemy fighters. The Belgians had just reformed above cloud after several pilots had chased some Me262s without result. At around 17.30, the squadron was close to Rheine aerodrome when P/O L. Lambrechts saw a Bf109 at about 600-700 feet. There was a dogfight going on and, as he went after the Bf109, the German pilot pulled up and went above the cloud, which was between 7-8/10ths at 5000 feet with clear patches. Lambrecht went after him and closed in to about 75-100 yards. He was dead astern when he opened fire with all guns. He saw strikes all over the cockpit and fuselage and the Bf109 rolled on its back and, smoking badly, dived vertically out of control. Soon after, Lambrecht saw two more Bf109s at 3000 feet. One of them was chasing F/Sgt C. Brahy. Quickly, he managed to get behind this Bf109 and opened fire from about 500 yards dead astern, closing until the enemy aircraft broke away. He saw strikes on the left wing. He could not go further because he had no ammunition left and also because another Bf109 was attacking him. He pulled up and left the area. Lambrechts claimed one Bf109 destroyed and another damaged on return, but his first was later adjusted to probably destroyed. He was not the only one to score in this engagement. Flight Lieutenant J. Lavigne did too, with one Bf109 destroyed, as did F/O A. Van Wersch, while Brahy claimed one damaged. The squadron returned to its armed recce work over the following days with an escort, that ended as a fighter sweep, thrown in for good measure. On 26 February 350 carried out Rhubarbs all day over the Rheine area, but their British CO was hit by flak and had to abandon his aircraft. He was a PoW for a short time as, five weeks later in March, he managed to escape and evade. The two ops on 1 March were uneventful. The next day, W/C G.C. Keefer and 350 participated in a fighter sweep over Rheine as the first operation of the day. German aircraft were reported by control, when the Wing was near Eschede, so the Spitfires turned towards Rheine. Wing Commander Keefer, who was flying with 130 Squadron, led them down while 350 remained as top cover. Keefer's formation was soon involved in a dogfight and the section led by F/L R. Hoornaert came to the rescue (Hoornaert was leading P/O L. Lambrechts, and Flight Sergeants J. Groensteen and F/Sgt E. Pauwels). Pauwels claimed a Bf109 as damaged while the other three put in claims for one destroyed each. The next day S/L Spencer's successor, S/L F.G. Woolley, arrived and was immediately on the job leading 350 in operations during the day and the busy few days that followed. On 13 March, he was leading an escort for Marauders when he saw a group of about twenty aircraft flying in the opposite direction. He went after them with his section and it took about two minutes at full throttle to catch up while still not being certain of their identity. He attempted to pull up alongside the outside aircraft on the right side. That aircraft turned into him and Woolley recognised it as a Fw190. Woolley got on to its tail and the Fw190 climbed up into a layer of thin cloud. He opened fire from dead astern at 100 yards, seeing many strikes on the wing roots and fuselage. The aircraft then burst into flames from the left wing root and base of the cockpit. Woolley had to break sharply away to avoid flying through debris. A few days later, 350 packed their things to return to England, to Warmwell, for an Air Firing course. They remained at Warmwell until 1 April, when released from the course, and were back at Eindhoven the next day. Their return coincided with S/L T. Spencer's homecoming after five weeks of captivity and an outstanding escape. On the 3rd, 350 took off twice for armed recces, but could not get through because of bad weather. The following day was most successful with an armed recce to Linden and Quakenbruck in the morning, during which a few lorries and horse carts were destroyed or damaged, and an armed recce mounted in the afternoon. Unfortunately, the flak was accurate and hit the Spitfire flown by F/L R. Hoornaert. He was obliged to make a forced landing near Meppen and spent what was left of the war as a PoW. The next day, the squadron returned to the same area. Flying Officer R. Muls, after having shot up a horse cart, was attacked by a Fw190 with a long nose. He avoided the initial attacked and got in position to fire at the Fw190D, seeing strikes on the fuselage. The Fw190 rolled on its back. Muls followed him, still firing, and was forced to break up to avoid a collision. He then received some backup from his wingman, F/Sgt S. Neulinger, who finished off the enemy aircraft, the German pilot eventually jumping out of his aircraft. The claim was shared by the two pilots. The Belgians returned with one of their own missing, however, as P/O A. Creswell-Turner had been shot down earlier, probably by the same Fw190D. The British pilot survived as a PoW. Two days later, 350 moved to Germany, B.106/Twente, from where operations began at once with patrols and armed recces. Flak remained the main danger and, in the Wihelmshaven-Emden area, F/Sgt G. Gigot was hit by flak. His wing exploded and his Glycol system began to leak, but, by some kind of miracle, he succeeded in returning close to base where the engine cut out and he landed a few hundred yards off the runway. Despite considerable damage, the Spitfire was repaired. Two days later it was the turn of P/O R. François to be hit by flak, receiving a 40mm shell in the fuselage. Like Gigot, he managed to reach base. On the 15th F/Sgt J. Van Liefland had to land at B.110, after his aircraft was hit by flak, but collided with an Auster. The aircraft was only good for scrap, but Van Leifland returned to the squadron. Previously, on 12 April, S/L Woolley had left to take command of 130 Squadron, allowing S/L Spencer to regain the position he had vacated in February when he was shot down. On 17 April, 350 made another move forward to B.118/Celle. This new base brought some luck for the Belgians when, after having seen one of their own lost in the morning (F/O M. Doncq was hit by flak, damaging an aileron, but he returned to base), F/Sgt A. Kicq shot down a Fw190D shortly after he bombed a tug southeast of Hamburg that afternoon. In the evening, the squadron performed a sweep over Berlin, but found little of interest if we ignore the symbolic side of the flight. Armed recces continued, mainly in the Lubeck-Hambourg area, and targets of opportunity were attacked when found. On 19 April, in the evening, 350 carried out a sweep over Parchim- Güstrow-Wismar. The CO was shot down while attacking a small ship in the bay off Wismar. His aircraft was seen to explode, but, miraculously, he was ejected by the explosion and a chute was seen to open (setting a record for surviving the lowest bale out on record – 30 feet). He landed in the water where he was rescued by German sailors and transported to a hospital where he spent the rest of the war. The squadron had its revenge the following day. It started badly for 350 as, during an armed recce over the Lubeck-Hamburg area in the late morning, F/L K. Smith (British) was shot down after flying into a flak trap. He was hit in the coolant system and made a forced landing near Schwerin. He was seen by his wingman, F/Sgt C. Orban de Xivry, getting out of the cockpit and walking towards the nearby woods. He evaded and returned to the squadron soon after on 4 May in a German staffcar. The blow was severe as in two days 350 had lost its CO and a Flight CO. The day was not over yet. Late in the evening, a sweep was flown in the Berlin area. In the Nauen area the formation encountered about twenty Fw190s flying in the opposite direction at a lower altitude. Combat was inevitable and the leader decided to attack with 350 immediately gaining the advantage over the Fw190s who lost five of their own to F/L D.R. Howorth, F/Sgt A. Kicq (and another probably destroyed), P/O R. Muls, F/O M. Doncq and P/O D.J. Watkins (British). However, two of the claims (Kicq's probably destroyed and Muls' victory) were later downgraded to damaged. The day ended much better than it started even if F/Sgt J. Groensteen was posted missing. The squadron's area of operations was restricted as the Soviets were entering Berlin for the final battle. All pilots received a special document, written in both English and Cyrillic, in case they had to make a forced landing in the Soviet lines. The next day, during a Wing sweep, led by G/C 'Johnnie' Johnson, 350 met Soviet aircraft for the first time (Yaks escorting the famous Shturmoviks). The squadron was led by the new CO, S/L H. Walmsley, who had just arrived from 130 Squadron. In the afternoon, while flying an armed recce in the Pritzwalk and Rostock area, F/O A. Van Eeckhoudt and P/O D.J. Watkins surprised a He111 heading north and following a road at ground level. Watkins was the first to attack, closing in and firing a quick burst at its left engine, which was hit. He had to break left to avoid debris. Albert

Spitfire NH689/MN-B at a snowy Y32/Ophoven in January 1945. It was S/L Spencer's mount at the time. The fuselage band has been overpainted to obey to the new 2 TAF regulation of 3 January 1945 but the underwing roundel has yet to be modified. *(André Bar)*

Squadron Leader Harold Walmsley in the cockpit of his aircraft. 'Harry' Walmsley joined the RAF in December 1940. However, he had to wait some months to commence flying training, being one of the first pupils to be sent to Rhodesia. He returned to the UK in June where he attended 61 OTU. In September, he was posted to 611 (County of Lincolnshire) Squadron as a NCO. In August 1943 he was posted to 132 (City of Bombay) Squadron as a flight commander where he was awarded the DFC and completed his tour in April 1944. He returned to operations in October 1944 with 130 (Punjab) Squadron, now flying the Griffon-powered Spitfire Mk.XIV. In April 1945, he was given command of 350 (Belgian) Squadron, the unit with which he made his final claims. The very last one, a Fw190 shared destroyed on 26 April, brought his score to eleven confirmed victories (one shared), one probable and four damaged. In July 1945, he added a Bar to his DFC. He continued to serve in the RAF until 1971 when he retired as a Group Captain. *(André Bar)*

Van Eeckhout followed and fired a long burst. The He111 then crash landed in a nearby field. The claim was shared. Later in the evening, the new CO was leading six aircraft on a fighter sweep over the Wismar-Parchim area when, approaching Wismar at 6000 feet, enemy aircraft were reported on the reciprocal heading at 7000 feet. They managed to get around behind the formation and started the chase. The enemy aircraft climbed into cloud and Walmsley ordered one of his sections to go above the cloud while he led his section into cloud. Walmsley found one Fw190 ahead of him. When the German realised he was being chased he dived through cloud to about 3500 feet. Walmsley followed it and fired two long-range bursts, but did not notice any results. At 2000 feet the Fw190 levelled out, slowed down and lowered its undercarriage as it approached Kleinen airfield. Walmsley got on its tail and fired a two second burst from directly astern. The Fw190 blew up and crashed in flames. Flight Lieutenant G. de Patoul claimed another Fw190 probably destroyed, but fell victim to an engine failure and had to abandon his aircraft. Captured, he was the last of the squadron's wartime losses. During the last days of April 1945, pressure was increased and as many armed recces as possible were flown as Nazi Germany collapsed. As each hour passed, however, the area to attack became more and more restricted as the Soviets advanced towards the west and the Allied lines. Despite this the Luftwaffe was continuing to fight and encounters became more frequent as German airspace shrunk. Around midday, during an armed recce, about twenty Fw190s were encountered around the airfield of Rechlin and, without difficulty, 350 claimed three destroyed, including two by P/O E. Pauwels, while F/O P. Delorme claimed another damaged, the third Fw190 destroyed being credited to the CO. The next day, the squadron scored again against Fw190s. Flight Sergeant G. Gigot sealed the fate of one while a second was shared by a group of four pilots that included the CO. This Fw190 was credited without the four pilots having to fire a single shot as it stalled as it tried to escape, the German pilot jumping out while his aircraft spun and crashed into the ground. Patrols and armed recces continued over the following days and were uneventful until the last the day of the month. That day the squadron patrolled in the Wittenburg-Haguenau-Ludwiglust area. Around 10.45, the patrol – consisting of F/L P. Bangerter (British), P/O D.J. Watkins and F/Sgt G. Gigot – caught roughly twenty Fw190s about to land in an airstrip. Carnage followed as the German fighters were caught low and slow. Bangerter claimed two, as did Watkins, while F/Sgt Gigot destroyed one and a sixth was shared between the three pilots. That's how April, with the squadron flying 550 sorties for the month, ended.

By May, it was clear the war in Europe was in its last days, but encounters with the Luftwaffe continued. On 1 May, 28 patrols were flown and in the evening, near Schwerin Lake, about twenty enemy aircraft were sighted flying at zero feet. Not identified at first, the Belgians, led by F/L R. Muls, came down from 10,000 feet to confirm a formation of Fw190s flying in sections of three. Flying Officer P. Leva selected the leading section and lined up the aircraft flying on the left side. He overshot owing to his diving speed, however, but, after climbing slightly to lose speed, he came in again behind the same Fw190. When within 300 yards, he fired a half second burst from 10° deflection without noticing any strikes. At the same time he observed he was closer to the middle aircraft of the section, so he got in behind it and fired a three second burst from 150 yards dead astern. He saw two explosions, one on each side of the fuselage. The Fw190 started to climb steeply to the right and Leva followed it and saw the German pilot jettison his hood, roll the aircraft on its back, and bale out at 1000 feet. Leva was the first to make a claim, but he was soon followed by F/Sgt H. Boels, who made two, and F/L R. Muls (one). The next day, an Arado 234 jet bomber was caught by surprise, as it was landing at Hohn aerodrome, and was shot down. Its destruction was shared by the four pilots of the section. This was the squadron's final aerial victory. Later in the evening, F/O P. Leva came close to being the unit's last casualty when he was hit by flak and the Spitfire caught fire. Miraculously, the fire went out and Leva was able to make it back to base safely. Patrols and armed recces continued over the next three days. The last were completed in the early hours of the 5th with no further ops necessary as the German forces in the north had capitulated on the 4th (effective from the 5th at 08.00). The squadron moved to B.152/Fassberg the next day. It stayed in Germany to become part of the occupying forces, moving to B.72/Husum on 21 June, B.116/Wunstorf on 13 July, and returning to B.152 Fassberg on 29 November. During that period of time, air activity was reduced, but two Spitfires were wrecked, the first on 9 June 1945 when the engine caught fire on start up, and the second on 17 December when it swung on take off onto soft ground and tipped over. The aircraft was not repaired as the RAF had too many Spitfires with the MUs. The Belgians swapped their Mk.XIVs for XVIs in August 1946, but that was not the end of the connection between 350 Squadron and the Spitfire XIV. After the war the new *Force Aérienne Belge* purchased 132 Spitfire XIVs from British stocks, to equip its fighter squadrons, to continue the story...

SECRET   PERSONAL COMBAT REPORT   REF:OPFLASH I25/2/I6.

Date:	May/2/I945.
Squadron:	350 (Belgian)
Type and mark of aircraft:	Spitfire XIV B.
Time up and down:	I631-I8I3.
Time of attack:	I7IO.
Place of attack:	Hohn aerodrome.
Height of enemy aircraft on first sighting	I000ft.
Own height on first sighting:	8000 ft.
Was cine gun used?	Yes.
Was gyro sight used?	No,not fitted.
Our casualties:	Nil.
Enemy casualties:	I Arado 234 destroyed shared by P/O Watkins/F/L Bangerter, F/O Van Eckhoudt and F/S Kicq

107 D
END
397/N

P/O WATKINS states:

I was leading Flounder section of 6 a/c on an armed recce in the RENDSBERG area. At about I7IO hrs whilst flying at 8000 ft, I saw in the circuit of HOHN aerodrome, a jet aircraft which I identified as an Arado 234 going in to land.

I dived from 8000 ft followed by the rest of the section, closed to within 50 yards behind E/A, and sprayed the mainplane and side of fuselage with machine gun fire. I broke away port as I saw aircraft smoking.

Pink 3 (F/L Bangerter) states:

I followed after Pink I and chased E/A as it was crossing aerodrome boundary at 200 ft approximately. E/A turned port away from the aerodrome with flaps and u/c down. I followed and fired cannon with a 5º angle deflection, and obtained strikes on port wing root and port engine, saw flames. I then broke port.

Pink 2 (F/S Kicq) and Pink 4 (F/O Van Eckhoudt) state that they made simultaneous deflection attacks, saw strikes and had to break away because of overtaking speed. Five seconds later, E/A flipped on its back, port mainplane fell off, and E/A struck the ground in a ball of fire.

We claim this Arado 234 destroyed.

Signature of Pink leader   _______________

Signature of Pink 2   _______________

Signature of Pink 3   _______________

Signature of Pink 4   _______________

Signature of Intelligence Officer   _______________

Date	Pilot	SN	Origin	Type	Serial	Code	Nb	Cat.
15.08.44	Sgt Hendrik **Boels**	RAF No. 1424945	(BEL)/RAF	*V-1*	**RM748**	MN-Z	0.5	C
	F/O Robert **Vanderveken**	RAF No. 147775	(BEL)/RAF		**RM655**	MN-X	0.5	C
16.08.44	F/Sgt Louis **Verbeeck**	RAF No. 1299865	(BEL)/RAF	*V-1*	**RM655**	MN-X	1.0	C
	P/O Jean **Lavigne**	RAF No. 156374	(BEL)/RAF	*V-1*	**RM701**	MN-O	0.5	C
	Sgt Paul **Leva**	RAF No. 1299863	(BEL)/RAF		**RM693**	MN-S	0.5	C
19.08.44	F/L André **Plisnier**	RAF No. 100654	(BEL)/RAF	Ju188	**RM754**	MN-G	1.0	C
	F/O Jacques **Wustefeld**	RAF No. 169984	(BEL)/RAF	*V-1*	**RM760**	MN-E	1.0	C
	F/Sgt Louis **Verbeeck**	RAF No. 1299865	(BEL)/RAF	*V-1*	**RM760**	MN-E	1.0	C
20.08.44	Sgt Paul **Leva**	RAF No. 1299863	(BEL)/RAF	*V-1*	**RM701**	MN-O	1.0	C
21.02.45	P/O Ludovic **Lambrechts**	RAF No. 186091	(BEL)/RAF	Bf109	**RM618**	MN-P	1.0	P
	F/L Jean **Lavigne**	RAF No. 156374	(BEL)/RAF	Bf109	**RM729**	MN-M	1.0	C
	P/O Albert **Van Wersch**	RAF No. 169983	(BEL)/RAF	Bf109	**RM648**	MN-R	1.0	C
02.03.45	P/O Ludovic **Lambrechts**	RAF No. 186091	(BEL)/RAF	Bf109	**RM618**	MN-P	1.0	C
	F/Sgt Jacques **Groensteen**	RAF No. 1299851	(BEL)/RAF	Bf109	**RM648**	MN-R	1.0	C
	F/L Roger **Hoornaert**	RAF No. 128392	(BEL)/RAF	Bf109	**RB183**	MN-Z	1.0	C
13.03.45	S/L Frank G. **Woolley**	RAF No. 105174	RAF	Fw190	**NH686**	MN-V	1.0	C
05.04.45	F/O Robert **Muls**	RAF No. 153066	(BEL)/RAF	Fw190	**RB189**	MN-G	0.50	C
	F/Sgt Sigmund**Neulinger**	RAF No. 1424916	(BEL)/RAF	Fw190	**RB181**	MN-H	0.50	C
17.04.45	F/Sgt André **Kicq**	RAF No. 1424884	(BEL)/RAF	Fw190	**RB155**	MN-C	1.0	C
20.04.45	F/L David M. **Howorth**	RAF No. 82678	RAF	Fw190	**RM618**	MN-P	1.0	C
	F/O Marcel **Doncq**	RAF No. 182304	(BEL)/RAF	Fw190	**NH693**	MN-J	1.0	C
	F/Sgt André **Kicq**	RAF No. 1424884	(BEL)/RAF	Fw190	**RB181**	MN-H	1.0	C
	P/O Desmond J. **Watkins**	RAF No. 188502	RAF	Fw190	**RB155**	MN-C	1.0	C
24.04.45	F/O Albert **Van Eeckhoudt**	RAF No. 158777	(BEL)/RAF	He111	**NH697**	MN-K	0.50	C
	P/O Desmond J. **Watkins**	RAF No. 188502	RAF				0.50	C
	S/L Harold E. **Walmsley**	RAF No. 139425	RAF	Fw190	**SM825**	MN-M	1.0	C
	F/L Guy **de Patoul**	RAF No. 87684	(BEL)/RAF	Fw190	**RM618**	MN-P	1.0	P
25.04.45	S/L Harold E. **Walmsley**	RAF No. 139425	RAF	Fw190	**SM825**	MN-M	1.0	C
	P/O Émile **Pauwels**	RAF No. 195058	(BEL)/RAF	Fw190	**NH654**	MN-X	2.0	C
26.04.45	F/Sgt Guy **Gigot**	RAF No. 1424921	(BEL)/RAF	Fw190	**RB181**	MN-H	1.0	C
	S/L Harold E. **Walmsley**	RAF No. 139425	RAF	Fw190	**RN198**	MN-T	0.25	C
	F/Sgt Guy **Gigot**	RAF No. 1424921	(BEL)/RAF		**RB181**	MN-H	0.25	C
	P/O Paul **Leva**	RAF No. 186344	(BEL)/RAF				0.25	C
	F/O Marcel **Doncq**	RAF No. 182304	(BEL)/RAF	Fw190	**NH693**	MN-J	0.25	C
30.04.45	F/L Patrick M. **Bangerter**	RAF No. 124911	RAF	Fw190	**SM825**	MN-M	2.0	C
	P/O Desmond J. **Watkins**	RAF No. 188502	RAF	Fw190	**SM814**	MN-A	2.0	C
	F/Sgt Guy **Gigot**	RAF No. 1424921	(BEL)/RAF	Fw190	**NH689**	MN-B	1.0	C
	F/L Patrick M. **Bangerter**	RAF No. 124911	RAF	Fw190	**SM825**	MN-M	0.33	C
	P/O Desmond J. **Watkins**	RAF No. 188502	RAF	Fw190	**SM814**	MN-A	0.33	C
	F/Sgt Guy **Gigot**	RAF No. 1424921	(BEL)/RAF	Fw190	**NH689**	MN-B	0.33	C
01.05.45	P/O Paul **Leva**	RAF No. 186344	(BEL)/RAF	Fw190	**NH690**	MN-R	1.0	C
	F/Sgt Hendrik **Boels**	RAF No. 1424945	(BEL)/RAF	Fw190	**RM689**	MN-E	2.0	C
	F/L Robert **Muls**	RAF No. 153066	(BEL)/RAF	Fw190	**SM825**	MN-M	1.0	C
02.05.45	F/L Patrick M. **Bangerter**	RAF No. 124911	RAF	Ar234	**NH661**	MN-Y	0.25	C
	P/O Desmond J. **Watkins**	RAF No. 188502	RAF		**SM814**	MN-A	0.25	C
	F/O Albert **Van Eeckhoudt**	RAF No. 158777	(BEL)/RAF		**NH697**	MN-K	0.25	C
	F/Sgt André **Kicq**	RAF No. 1424884	(BEL)/RAF		**RB155**	MN-C	0.25	C

Total: 33.0 + 6 V-1s

Some of the pilots of 350 Sqn who made claims during the final stages of the war. Above:

F/L D.M. Howorth, a British pilot, as was P/O D.J. Watkins. Both arrived at the squadron in March 1945 to reinforce the Belgians. Watkins had previously served with 132 Sqn. He was awarded the DFC in July 1945 for his service with 350.
Three Belgian pilots. Left, Pilot Officer E. Pauwels, who fled Belgium in March 1941, but was interned in Spain until March 1942 before making for the UK. He was posted to 350 Sqn in July 1944 as his first operational assignment. He survived the war. Flight Sergeant A. Kicq (below left) arrived at the squadron two weeks after Pauwels. He managed to escape Belgium in October 1941 and arrived in England in March 1942. Joining 350 Sqn in July 1944, he survived the war. Both flew for the Belgian airline SABENA after the war. Below right, Flight Sergeant 'Kéké' Gigot. He reached England in March 1942 after having been interned in Spain for six months. He would joined SABENA airlines as well after the war. *(André Bar)*

Date	Pilot	S/N	Origin	Serial	Code	Fate
01.09.44	*Destroyed by V-1 on the ground*	-	-	**RM695**	MN-S	-
25.10.44	F/Sgt Ludovic **Lambrechts**	RAF No. 1899871	(bel)/RAF	**RM615**		-
04.11.44	S/L Léopold **Collignon**	RAF No. 116288	(bel)/RAF	**NH716**	MN-X	-
14.11.44	F/O Ferdinand **Verpoorten**	RAF No. 169600	(bel)/RAF	**RM671**		-
08.12.44	F/Sgt Robert **Jaminé**	RAF No. 1424883	(bel)/RAF	**RB145**		-
18.12.44	F/L Roger **Hoornaert**	RAF No. 128392	(bel)/RAF	**RM691**	MN-Q	-
24.12.44	S/L Léopold **Collignon**	RAF No. 116288	(bel)/RAF	**RM690**		**Inj.**
25.12.44	F/O Jacob **Vanderperren**	RAF No. 120896	(bel)/RAF	**RM673**	MN-K	†
01.01.45	*Destroyed in air raid*	-	-	**RM622**		-
16.01.45	F/L Herman **Smets**	RAF No. 87694	(bel)/RAF	**RM619**	MN-D	**PoW**
23.01.45	F/Sgt Robert **Huens**	RAF No. 1899804	(bel)/RAF	**NH711**		†
11.02.45	F/Sgt Joseph **Laloux**	RAF No. 1299839	(bel)/RAF	**NH685**		**PoW**
26.02.45	S/L Terence **Spencer**	RAF No. 47269	RAF	**RM739**	MN-H	**Eva.**
04.04.45	F/L Roger **Hoornaert**	RAF No. 128392	(bel)/RAF	**RB183**	MN-Z	**PoW**
05.04.45	P/O Anthony **Cresswell-Turner**	RAF No. 152668	RAF	**RB185**	MN-L	**PoW**
15.04.45	F/Sgt Jacob **Vanliefland**	RAF No. 1424983	(bel)/RAF	**SM830**		-
19.04.45	S/L Terence **Spencer**	RAF No. 47269	RAF	**SM814**	MN-A	**PoW**
20.04.45	F/L Kenneth **Smith**	RAF No. 115521	RAF	**RM744**	MN-L	**Eva.**
	F/Sgt Jacques **Groensteen**	RAF No. 1299851	(bel)/RAF	**NH686**	MN-V	†
24.04.45	F/L Guy **de Patoul**	RAF No. 87684	(bel)/RAF	**RM618**	MN-P	**PoW**

Total: 20

Date	Pilot	S/N	Origin	Serial	Code	Fate
27.08.44	F/Sgt Joseph **Laloux**	RAF No. 1299839	(bel)/RAF	**RM751**	MN-T	-
11.11.44	F/Sgt Mathieu **Morel**	RAF No. 1424812	(bel)/RAF	**RB168**	MN-X	†
09.06.45	F/O Guy **de Bueger**	RAF No. 130772	(bel)/RAF	**RM869**	MN-V	-
17.12.45	F/Sgt Gaston **de Gerlache de G.**	RAF No. 1814881	(bel)/RAF	**NH660**	MN-S	-

Total: 4

Various scenes of 350 Sqn while it was part of the occupying forces in Germany. Above, some Spitfire XIVs lined-up and, below, Spitfire XIV MN-Z (probably RB180) parked behind a captured Fieseler 156. These photos were taken at Fassberg during the summer of 1945. *(André Bar)*

Spitfire MV267 was issued to 350 Sqn in mid-June 1945. It was part of the last batch with the new canopy and carried the two 0.50-in machine gun armament.
Below, Spitfire RN198/MN-T, received in July 1945, with the classic canopy.
(André Bar)

Victories - confirmed or probable claims: 119.0 V-1s

First operational sortie:
24.04.44
Last operational sortie:
10.08.44

Number of sorties: *ca.* 2,575

Total aircraft written-off: 4

Aircraft lost on operations: 3
Aircraft lost in accidents: 1

Squadron code letters:
VL & 3W

COMMANDING OFFICERS

| Maj Keith C. KUHLMANN | SAAF No. P102441 | SAAF | ... | ... |

SQUADRON USAGE

After flying the ageing Spitfire Mk.V for about nine months (see *SQUADRONS! 30*), it was time for the Dutch to change mounts. The latest mark, the Mk.XIV, had recently been introduced into service and the Dutch were pleased to know they would convert soon. To do so, they left Hawkinge for Ackington on 10 March under the supervision of Major K.C. Kuhlmann, the South African OC. The first Mk.XIV arrived the following day with F/L J.L. Plesman at the controls. The squadron, with the arrival of other aircraft, began the conversion, but it was a big step from the Mk.V to the XIV. An extensive ground school, therefore, was the first step. It is not until the 17th that the first test flight was undertaken, the CO having the privilege. The two flight commanders, Flight Lieutenants Plesman and van Eendenburg, followed suit the next day. In addition to the practice flights with the Mk.XIVs, the squadron continued to fly some operations with the old Mk.Vs. A drama occurred on 11 April when F/O J.W. van Hamel took off for an altitude test. He was seen, about 45 minutes after take off, to crash into a hillside southwest of Rothbury. While the cause of the crash was never determined, it was suspected he had experienced an oxygen failure. This, and some minor incidents, was the only major event of note before the squadron moved to 141 Airfield at Hartford Bridge with W/C Barthold as wing leader. The move took place on 23 April (RB141/L, RB158, RB160/VL-A, RB168, RB171/E, RB184/B, RB186, RB189). The next day the Dutch completed four scrambles, three to investigate unidentified aircraft and one to investigate a fighter in difficulty. The tasking for the Dutch was to prevent the Germans from taking high altitude photographs of the English coast. Unknown to the Dutch, D-Day was approaching and the extent of the preparations for the invasion had to be kept from the Germans as much as possible. The following days, more scrambles took place, but all were subsequently converted to defensive patrols. This remained the daily task for a few days. On the 27th F/O L.D. Wolters and F/O M.L. van Bergen closed on a German aircraft, but turned for home near Cherbourg while they still had enough fuel. By 30 April the squadron had already carried out about 100 standing defensive patrols (mainly over the Isle of Wight). In May, this number increased to 500, but the squadron lost two aircraft. The first loss occurred on 2 May when Sgt H.C.A. Roovers never returned from a patrol late in the evening. That evening, at 20.30, Black section (F/Sgt J.A. Maier and Sgt Roovers) was ordered to patrol the Isle of Wight. Roovers was following his leader in a wide echelon right until Maier gave another vector. He looked around to see if Roovers had followed correctly, but there was no sign of him and he did not respond to calls over the R/T. Maier continued the patrol until relieved. He had hoped Roovers had returned to base following a R/T failure, but that was not the case. With darkness approaching, it was too late to launch an ASR mission. One was performed in the early hours of the 3rd, but nothing was found. The routine continued until the 19th when a Ranger was flown in conjunction with 91 Squadron (also equipped with Spitfire XIVs) and W/C Oxspring. Each unit provided three Spitfires. The CO, with Flying Officers L.M. Meijers and J. Jonker, participated in the raid. Two other pilots, Flying Officers van Arkel and Muller, had to abandon the op after having trouble with their 90 gallon auxiliary tanks (they later flew a reconnaissance over Boulogne where they spotted a large

322 Sqn at Woodvale, England, in December 1943. Most of these pilots participated in the V-1 campaign a few months later:
Back row (left to right): Flight Sergeants J.H. Harms, C. Kooy (†28.01.45), W.H. Kuyper, and R.L. van Beers (PoW 26.08.44), P/O P.A. Cramerus, Flight Sergeants M.J. Janssen, J.A. Maier (†12.07.44), F.A. van Valkenburg, and W. de Vries, Flying Officers J. van Arkel, E.J. van Nagell (†28.01.44), C.R.R. Manders, and M.A. Muller.
Middle row (left to right): Flying Officers J.B.C.A. Arts and J.L. Flinterman, Flight Sergeants G.J.D. Dijkman and H.G. Roovers (†02.05.44), F/O F.J.A. van Eijk (†14.02.45), F/Sgt H.C. Cramm (†30.03.45), Flying Officers R.F. van Daalen Wetters and G.F.J. Jongbloed, F/Sgt J.C. van Roosendaal, Flying Officers J.W. van Hamel (†11.04.44), J. Jonker and L.D. Wolters (†16.09.44).
Front row (left to right): Flying Officers M.L. van Bergen, J.W. Dekker, and Schudel (Medical Officer), Flight Lieutenants W. de Wolff and J.L. Plesman, Maj. K.C. Kuhlmann (CO - SAAF) with 'Polly Grey' the mascot, Flight Lieutenants J.B. Niven (RAF), L.C.M. van Eendenburg, and L.E. Chiswell (Adj), P/O J.G. Lockton (IO), F/O L.M. Meyers. (*Collections Nederlands Instituut voor Militaire Historie - NIMH*)

ship and duly reported its sighting on return). The Spitfires flew to Ostend, then flew to the south of Antwerp, turned north, flew over the aerodrome of Volkel, but the Germans based there did not react even though the Spitfires went over at 3000 feet, and came out via Rotterdam. The next day, 322 returned to its routine patrols, but was plagued by various incidents, fortunately with only minor consequences for aircraft and pilots, until the 31st when the second loss of the month occurred. In the early hours of the day, F/O J.W. Dekker and F/Sgt C. Kooy took off on a patrol, but Kooy found his aircraft nose heavy and difficult to fly as he had to hold the stick with both hands. He immediately called his leader and told him he was going to land. The weather conditions were such, however, that he could not see the ground so he asked control for a homing, but then found he could not steer the course as his arms were so tired that he had to use his legs as well. His speed at that time was 120 mph and his height 250 feet and, having tried without success to make base for about fifteen minutes, he decided to climb and bale out, informing control of his decision. He climbed with difficulty to 1800 feet and baled out successfully, his chute opening at 900 feet. He saw the Spitfire crash in flames 300 yards away. It was not a good day for the Dutch as F/Sgt G.J.D. Dijkman's right undercarriage collapsed, causing the aircraft to loop to the right with the wing touching the ground. He escaped injury and the Spitfire was later repaired. The bad weather during the first days of June limited the number of patrols flown. On 5 June, during the day, stripes were painted on the aircraft and late in the evening W/C Oxspring announced, in the presence of all pilots and the CO, that D-Day, the first day of the long anticipated invasion and the start of the liberation of Europe, had been fixed for the next day. The new codes 3W were also painted on the aircraft. The squadron's task was to fly high altitude patrols. Oxspring defined the limits of the assault area and gave a general idea of the initial phase, pointing at a map of the region involved that comprised the Cherbourg Peninsula up to the east of Le Havre. The squadron was asked to be ready by 04.30 the next morning. Dawn on the 6th saw everyone ready at 04.30, with some concern as the night had been windy and rainy, but by 07.30 the sky seemed to have cleared enough. As far as 322 was concerned, however, nothing happened before 15.15 when the squadron completed uneventful anti-reconnaissance patrols over the Isle of Wight. The following day was even worse, with only a section scramble to investigate an unidentified aircraft that turned out to be a Mosquito, but on the other hand, the weather was not as good as expected. While the number of patrols almost returned to normal on the 8th, they soon stopped as the weather steadily deteriorated. The bad weather also prevented any flying the next day. Patrols resumed in earnest on the 10th. The nature of the sorties changed a little on the 12th when 322 was tasked with escorting five Dakotas towing Waco gliders to Sainte-Mère-Église on the Cherbourg Peninsula. This was completed without incident. Further escorts for transport aircraft were carried out over the next few days. Most of the time, the task was completed without incident, but on the 16th F/Sgt

Spitfire XIV NH700/VL-P being washed in April 1944. In the foreground, participating in the task, is F/L van Eendenburg, one of the two flight commanders at the time and who would later, in September 1944, take over 322 Sqn after Major Kuhlmann was shot down and made a PoW. 'Kees' van Eendenburg survived the war. Before joining 322, he served with Nos. 41, 167, 118 Squadrons. He was among the first Dutch to succeed escaping to England, after the occupation of the Netherlands, as early as July 1940. This airframe was lost soon after on the 11th during an air test killing the pilot, F/O J.W. van Hamel.

F.A. van Valkenburg was hit by flak and had to make an emergency landing on a strip in Normandy (B4). Two days later 322 received an unexpected new assignment – anti-Diver patrols (intercepting V-1 flying bombs that had begun to hit the British Isles). The area assigned to 322 was between Halsham and Battle. This new tasking was received with great satisfaction as the pilots felt that at last they would be able to use their cannons for the first time since conversion to the Spitfire XIV. The first anti-Diver patrols were flown on 18 June at 13.15. It did not take long before the Dutch opened their score against the pilotless machines as Flying Officers R.G. Burgwal and L.M. Meijers shot down a V-1 each in the middle of the afternoon. Rudi Burgwal got his V-1 by firing at it from 600 yards (it exploded) while Meijers attacked from 400 yards and watched it turn over and hit the ground. Later, in the evening, another V-1 was shared by F/L L.C.M. van Eendenburg and F/O R.F. van Daalen Wetters. The following day, 322 added four more V-1s to its tally (two were shared with aircraft from other units, the first with a Tempest, the second with a Spitfire). Until the end of the month, anti-Diver patrols increased significantly with no less than 62 sorties flown on 29 June from West Malling, the new station the squadron had been operating from since the 20th. At the same time, the score of V-1s increased too with one claimed on the 20th, one on the 21st, three on the 22nd (F/L J.L. Plesman claimed the first of his eleven destroyed), two on the 23rd

Among the Dutch pilots who moved to 322 from 167 Sqn was F/O Jan L. Plesman, who soon became a flight commander. Under training when the Netherlands were invaded in May 1940, he managed to flee from his country at the end of September 1940 and travelled to France and Spain and Portugal. He enlisted in the RAF in August 1941 and served with 64 Sqn before joining 167 Sqn in July 1942. While he did not distinguish himself while flying the Spitfire V, he was successful against the V1s while flying the Spitfire XIV and became a V1 ace. He was later shot down and killed by flak on 1 September 1944.

In June 1944, 322 Sqn switched squadron codes from 'VL' to '3W', using the latter until the end of war. This is Major Kuhlmann's mount, NH718/3W-G, in full D-Day markings. He, Jongbloed and Burgwal were successful against V-1s while flying in this aircraft. *(M. Schoeman)*

(including one for the CO), and seven (one shared) on the 27th. Flight Sergeant J. Harms got two, but a third was disallowed and eventually credited to a Tempest pilot. This rate of scoring continued with four more on the 28th (one shared), nine on the 29th, and five on the 30th. These were good results, but it was a dangerous game as, on the 29th, F/Sgt W. de Vries came close to being shot down by flak while attacking a V-1. His right aileron was blown out and he received holes in the right wing, engine cowling and fuselage, forcing him to land at Kingsnorth.

July started with the destruction of another V-1 by W/O J.A. Maier. The next day, 322 could not fly because of a low ceiling, causing some frustration as the V-1s continued to hit the country. It was not until the evening that flying resumed. The same scenario was repeated on 3 July, but 322 was able to fly patrols a bit earlier, in the middle of the afternoon, and in the evening three V-1s were destroyed. July 4 was a normal day of operations with continuous patrols from 04.35 to 23.35 hours. Flying Officers J. Jonker, R.F. Burgwal and F.W. Speetjens added a V-1 each, but Speetjens had a misadventure, when his engine cut two minutes after having destroyed the V-1, and he had to make a belly landing in a wheat field at Hever. He was not injured and the aircraft not seriously damaged. The next day, F/Sgt M.J. Janssen and F/L L.C.M. van Eendenburg claimed two V-1s each, but those were soon reduced to one and a half each, Janssen having to share his V-1 with a 1 Squadron Spitfire and van Eendenburg with a Polish pilot from 316 Squadron. Bad luck continued the next day when the claim made by F/Sgt H. Cram was disallowed. The Dutch got their revenge on the 7th when they claimed six V-1s destroyed, all being allowed. Among the victors was F/O Rudi Burgwal who had a narrow escape when his target exploded in mid-air after he had closed in from 200 yards to 100 yards. He made an emergency landing at Ashford. On the 8th 322 flew its first night sortie during which F/Sgt Cram destroyed a Diver at around 04.30 hours. During the day, seven more followed, including five for Burgwal alone! The next day Cram claimed two V-1s in three minutes. Flying continued after midnight and at 00.20 on the 10th F/L Plesman shot down a V-1. Flight Lieutenant van Eendenburg added another in the afternoon. The next day, five more were credited to five different Dutch pilots, followed by another five, and a sixth shared with a USAAF Mustang, the next day. The latter caused the death of a Dutchman, W/O J. Maier, when the flying bomb he was trying to tip with his wing was shot down by the Mustang. The Spitfire was caught in the explosion and it fell out of control and crashed. On the 13th, Flight Sergeants M.J. Janssen and J.H. Harms got one Diver each, but unfortunately the weather stopped the hunt prematurely around teatime. The weather remained fine on the 14th and four more V-1s were shot down by the Dutch, including two by F/L Plesman. The squadron scored two on the 16th, three on the 18th and another six on the 19th even though one had to be shared with another squadron. Plesman and F/O Burgwal, the top scorers of the squadron, were among the claimants. The next day, Plesman was patrolling Margate to Folkestone when he was told a Diver was coming in near Dover. He spotted it and attacked from 150 yards line astern. He saw strikes and the flying bomb crashed and exploded northeast of Ashford to make his eighth claim over a V-1. Less than an hour later, it was the turn of F/O M.L. van Bergen to score. On 22 July, the squadron moved to the advanced landing ground at Deanland, west of Hailsham, and, from the new base, 322 destroyed three more V-1s that day (including two for Burgwal). The next day Flying Officers G.F.J Jongbloed and C.R.R. Manders added a Diver each to their tally. One was claimed on the 24th, shared by Burgwal and F/O J. Jonker, and another five (two being shared with other squadrons) followed on the 26th. Burgwal was once again in the mix. The squadron was now approaching the 100-kill mark and the question was who would claim it. On the 28th two V-1s were destroyed, one being credited to the South African CO, and two more were added to the tally on the 29th. A single victory on the 30th brought the score to 99. Everybody was expecting the 100th to be claimed the next day, but the weather prevented any flying! That's how July ended, a month that saw the completion of no less than 1026 sorties.

The day everyone was waiting for came on 2 August. The previous bad weather also prevented any flying before 17.00 hours, but no Diver was seen. The achievement of the century was made in a strange manner as the two claims made by F/Sgt R.L. van Beers

at 12.54 and 13.00 respectively near the Tunbridge Wells area had to be shared, the first with a 3 Squadron Tempest and the second with the pilot of a 91 Squadron Spitfire XIV. The two half claims could not count for a full claim so negotiations were opened with 91 Squadron with a view to asking them to give up the half share. Flight Lieutenant R.S. Nash, of 91 Squadron, generously withdrew his half claim making van Beers the pilot who claimed the 100th flying bomb for the Dutch. The squadron had to wait until the 4th to score again, Flight Lieutenants J. van Arkel and J.F. Plesman shooting down one V-1 each. The day before, 322 had received some ten new Spitfire XIVs armed with two 0.50-in machine guns instead of the outdated four 0.303-in armament. Further aircraft followed over the next few days. The squadron's scoreboard was increased by three more V-1s on 5 August (two for F/O R.F. Burgwal's account), one on 6 August, another on the night of 7 August, and a single night kill late on the 8th. The same day 322 was notified it would exchange the Spitfire XIVs for Spitfire IXs in order to carry out another task. This could have been the last of the V-1 claims, but while the squadron was released from dawn on the 9th until 12.30 on the 10th, F/L Plesman made three anti-Diver patrols that night, the first between 22.30 and 24.00, the second from 01.00 to 02.50, and the last one between 04.30 and 05.30. Eight minutes after taking off for his third night patrol, Plesman was warned a Diver was approaching and he was vectored to the interception. He attacked line astern from a range of 200 yards. He saw strikes and it exploded on the ground in an open field. This was the last V-1 destroyed by the Dutch. More than 250 sorties were flown by the Spitfire XIVs in August. On the 11th, in the middle of the afternoon, operations on the Spitfire IX began. (see *SQUADRONS! 45*)

Two Dutch V-1 aces:
Left, Gerald F.J. Jongbloed served with 131 Sqn before joining 322. He later flew Tempests with 222 Sqn where he made his last V-1 claim. He survived the war. *(A.Thomas)*
Below, Jan van Arkel reached England as early as May 1940. After a short spell as a driver for the Dutch defence minister in London, he enlisted in the RAF in March 1941. After his training was completed, he was posted to 41 Sqn and then joined the Dutch flight of 167 Sqn, which became 322 Sqn in June 1943. He survived the war and continued his military career in the new RNethAF until 1974.
(Collections Nederlands Instituut voor Militaire Historie - NIMH)

Date	Pilot	SN	Origin	Type	Serial	Code	Nb	Cat.
18.06.44	F/O Rudolph **Burgwal**	RAF No. 113893	(NL)/RAF	*V-1*		3W-K	1.0	C
	F/O Lourens **Meijers**	RAF No. 136569	(NL)/RAF	*V-1*	**NH686**	3W-M	1.0	C
	F/L Leendert van **Eendenburg**	RAF No. 108814	(NL)/RAF	*V-1*	**RB184**	3W-B	0.5	C
	F/O Rudolf van **Daalen Wetters**	RAF No.104590	(NL)/RAF			3W-K	0.5	C
19.06.44	F/O Rudolph **Burgwal**	RAF No. 113893	(NL)/RAF	*V-1*		3W-D	0.5	C
	F/O Pieter **Cramerus**	RAF No. 143220	(NL)/RAF	*V-1*		3W-N	1.0	C
	F/O Jan **Dekker**	RAF No. 135761	(NL)/RAF	*V-1*		3W-U	1.0	C
	F/O Gerard **Jongbloed**	RAF No. 104592	(NL)/RAF	*V-1*	**RB184**	3W-B	0.5	C
20.06.44	F/L Leendert van **Eendenburg**	RAF No. 108814	(NL)/RAF	*V-1*	**RB184**	3W-B	1.0	C
21.06.44	F/Sgt Ronald van **Beers**	RAF No. 1814965	(NL)/RAF	*V-1*		3W-K	1.0	C
22.06.44	F/L Jan **Plesman**	RAF No. 102524	(NL)/RAF	*V-1*		3W-V	1.0	C
	F/O Coenraad **Manders**	RAF No. 113889	(NL)/RAF	*V-1*		3W-U	1.0	C
	F/O Rudolf van **Daalen Wetters**	RAF No.104590	(NL)/RAF	*V-1*		3W-J	1.0	C
23.06.44	F/O Jan van **Arkel**	RAF No. 124639	(NL)/RAF	*V-1*		3W-V	0.50	C
	F/O Mijnard van **Bergen**	RAF No. 113896	(NL)/RAF			3W-N	0.50	C
	Maj Keith C. **Kuhlmann**	SAAF No. P102441	SAAF	*V-1*	**NH718**	3W-G	1.0	C
27.06.44	F/Sgt Ronald van **Beers**	RAF No. 1814965	(NL)/RAF	*V-1*		3W-H	1.0	C
	F/Sgt Cornelis **Kooy**	RAF No. 1814967	(NL)/RAF	*V-1*	**RM678**	3W-Q	0.50	C
	F/Sgt Johannes **Harms**	RAF No. 1814945	(NL)/RAF	*V-1*		3W-J	2.0	C
	F/L Jan **Plesman**	RAF No. 102524	(NL)/RAF	*V-1*		3W-V	1.0	C
	F/O Mijnard van **Bergen**	RAF No. 113896	(NL)/RAF	*V-1*		3W-N	1.0	C
	F/O Jan van **Arkel**	RAF No. 124639	(NL)/RAF	*V-1*		3W-T	1.0	C
28.06.44	F/O Lambert **Wolters**	RAF No. 141896	(NL)/RAF	*V-1*		3W-N	0.50	C
	W/O Justin **Maier**	RAF No. 1549995	(NL)/RAF	*V-1*	**RM678**	3W-Q	1.0	C
	F/O Gerard **Jongbloed**	RAF No. 104592	(NL)/RAF	*V-1*		3W-C	1.0	C
	F/Sgt Frederik van **Valkenburg**	RAF No. 1814944	(NL)/RAF	*V-1*	**NH649**	3W-F	1.0	C
29.06.44	F/O Frans **Speetjens**	RAF No. 145140	(NL)/RAF	*V-1*		3W-J	1.0	C
	F/O Gerard **Jongbloed**	RAF No. 104592	(NL)/RAF	*V-1*		3W-K	1.0	C
	F/Sgt Martin **Janssen**	RAF No. 1814942	(NL)/RAF	*V-1*		3W-D	1.0	C
	F/O Rudolph **Burgwall**	RAF No. 113893	(NL)/RAF	*V-1*	**NH649**	3W-F	2.0	C
	F/O Martin **Muller**	RAF No. 135760	(NL)/RAF	*V-1*		3W-T	1.0	C
	F/L Jan **Plesman**	RAF No. 102524	(NL)/RAF	*V-1*		3W-W	1.0	C
	F/O Lambert **Wolters**	RAF No. 141896	(NL)/RAF	*V-1*		3W-N	1.0	C
	F/O Frans van **Eijk**	RAF No.113894	(NL)/RAF	*V-1*	**NH699**	3W-R	1.0	C
	F/Sgt Willem de **Vries**	RAF No. 1814947	(NL)/RAF	*V-1*	**RM678**	3W-Q	1.0	C
30.06.44	F/O Lourens **Meijers**	RAF No. 136569	(NL)/RAF	*V-1*		3W-J	1.0	C
	F/O Jan van **Arkel**	RAF No. 124639	(NL)/RAF	*V-1*		3W-D	1.0	C
	F/O Rudolph **Burgwal**	RAF No. 113893	(NL)/RAF	*V-1*	**RB171**	3W-E	2.0	C
	F/O Jan **Jonker**	RAF No. 132082	(NL)/RAF	*V-1*		3W-K	1.0	C
01.07.44	W/O Justin **Maier**	RAF No. 1549995	(NL)/RAF	*V-1*		3W-T	1.0	C
03.07.44	F/Sgt Frederik **Cramm**	RAF No. 1692491	(NL)/RAF	*V-1*	**NH699**	3W-R	1.0	C
	F/O Jan **Jonker**	RAF No. 132082	(NL)/RAF	*V-1*	**RB160**	3W-A	1.0	C
	F/O Frans van **Eijk**	RAF No.113894	(NL)/RAF	*V-1*		3W-U	0.5	C
	P/O Aart **Homburg**	RAF No.125169	(NL)/RAF			3W-Y	0.5	C
04.07.44	F/O Jan **Jonker**	RAF No. 132082	(NL)/RAF	*V-1*		3W-D	1.0	C
	F/O Rudolph **Burgwal**	RAF No. 113893	(NL)/RAF	*V-1*	**NH649**	3W-F	1.0	C
	F/O Frans **Speetjens**	RAF No. 145140	(NL)/RAF	*V-1*	**RB160**	3W-A	1.0	C
05.07.44	F/Sgt Martin **Janssen**	RAF No. 1814942	(NL)/RAF	*V-1*		3W-D	1.5	C
	F/L Leendert van **Eendenburg**	RAF No. 108814	(NL)/RAF	*V-1*	**RB184**	3W-B	1.5	C
07.07.44	F/O Rudolph **Burgwall**	RAF No. 113893	(NL)/RAF	*V-1*		3W-C	1.0	C
	F/Sgt Cornelis **Kooy**	RAF No. 1814967	(NL)/RAF	*V-1*		3W-N	1.0	C

Date	Name	Service No.	Unit	Type	Aircraft	Code	Score	Cat.
	F/Sgt Gerard **Dijkman**	RAF No. 1814946	(NL)/RAF	*V-1*		3W-Y	1.0	C
	F/O Martin **Muller**	RAF No. 135760	(NL)/RAF	*V-1*		3W-W	1.0	C
	W/O Justin **Maier**	RAF No. 1549995	(NL)/RAF	*V-1*	NH686	3W-M	1.0	C
	F/O Pieter **Cramerus**	RAF No. 143220	(NL)/RAF	*V-1*		3W-V	1.0	C
08.07.44	F/Sgt Frederik **Cramm**	RAF No. 1692491	(NL)/RAF	*V-1*		3W-T	1.0	C
	F/O Rudolph **Burgwal**	RAF No. 113893	(NL)/RAF	*V-1*	NH718	3W-G	4.5	C
	F/O Jan **Jonker**	RAF No. 132082	(NL)/RAF	*V-1*		3W-K	1.0	C
	F/L Leendert van **Eendenburg**	RAF No. 108814	(NL)/RAF	*V-1*	RB184	3W-B	1.0	C
09.07.44	F/Sgt Frederik **Cramm**	RAF No. 1692491	(NL)/RAF	*V-1*	NH699	3W-R	2.0	C
10.07.44	F/L Jan **Plesman**	RAF No. 102524	(NL)/RAF	*V-1*		3W-W	1.0	C
	F/L Leendert van **Eendenburg**	RAF No. 108814	(NL)/RAF	*V-1*	RB184	3W-B	1.0	C
11.07.44	F/O Lourens **Meijers**	RAF No. 136569	(NL)/RAF	*V-1*		3W-H	1.0	C
	F/O Martin **Muller**	RAF No. 135760	(NL)/RAF	*V-1*		3W-T	1.0	C
	F/O Coenraad **Manders**	RAF No. 113889	(NL)/RAF	*V-1*		3W-V	1.0	C
	F/O Frans van **Eijk**	RAF No.113894	(NL)/RAF	*V-1*		3W-U	1.0	C
	W/O Justin **Maier**	RAF No. 1549995	(NL)/RAF	*V-1*	NH686	3W-M	1.0	C
12.07.44	F/O Coenraad **Manders**	RAF No. 113889	(NL)/RAF	*V-1*		3W-V	1.0	C
	F/Sgt Martin **Janssen**	RAF No. 1814942	(NL)/RAF	*V-1*	RB171	3W-E	2.0	C
	F/O Johannes **Vlug**	RAF No. 145141	(NL)/RAF	*V-1*	RB160	3W-A	1.0	C
	F/O Gerard **Jongbloed**	RAF No. 104592	(NL)/RAF	*V-1*	NH718	3W-G	1.0	C
	W/O Justin **Maier**	RAF No. 1549995	(NL)/RAF	*V-1*	RM678	3W-Q	0.5	C
13.07.44	F/Sgt Martin **Janssen**	RAF No. 1814942	(NL)/RAF	*V-1*	RB160	3W-A	1.0	C
	F/Sgt Johannes **Harms**	RAF No. 1814945	(NL)/RAF	*V-1*	RB141	3W-L	1.0	C
14.07.44	F/Sgt Ronald van **Beers**	RAF No. 1814965	(NL)/RAF	V-1		3W-H	1.0	C
	F/Sgt Martin **Janssen**	RAF No. 1814942	(NL)/RAF	V-1		3W-C	1.0	C
	F/L Jan **Plesman**	RAF No. 102524	(NL)/RAF	V-1		3W-W	2.0	C
16.07.44	F/O Gerard **Jongbloed**	RAF No. 104592	(NL)/RAF	*V-1*	NH718	3W-G	1.0	C
	F/O Jan van **Arkel**	RAF No. 124639	(NL)/RAF	*V-1*		3W-V	1.0	C
18.07.44	F/L Leendert van **Eendenburg**	RAF No. 108814	(NL)/RAF	*V-1*	RB160	3W-A	1.0	C
	F/O Johannes **Vlug**	RAF No. 145141	(NL)/RAF	*V-1*		3W-K	2.0	C
19.07.44	F/L Leendert van **Eendenburg**	RAF No. 108814	(NL)/RAF	*V-1*	RB184	3W-B	1.0	C
	F/O Gerard **Jongbloed**	RAF No. 104592	(NL)/RAF	*V-1*	RB171	3W-E	0.5	C
	F/O Johannes **Vlug**	RAF No. 145141	(NL)/RAF			3W-D	0.5	C
	F/O Rudolph **Burgwal**	RAF No. 113893	(NL)/RAF	*V-1*	NH649	3W-F	1.0	C
	F/L Jan **Plesman**	RAF No. 102524	(NL)/RAF	*V-1*		3W-W	1.0	C
	F/O Gerard **Jongbloed**	RAF No. 104592	(NL)/RAF	*V-1*	RB171	3W-E	1.0	C
	F/O Pieter **Cramerus**	RAF No. 143220	(NL)/RAF	*V-1*		3W-U	0.5	C
20.07.44	F/L Jan **Plesman**	RAF No. 102524	(NL)/RAF	*V-1*		3W-W	1.0	C
	F/O Mijnard van **Bergen**	RAF No. 113896	(NL)/RAF	*V-1*		3W-U	1.0	C
22.07.44	F/O Gerard **Jongbloed**	RAF No. 104592	(NL)/RAF	*V-1*	RB171	3W-E	1.0	C
	F/O Rudolph **Burgwal**	RAF No. 113893	(NL)/RAF	*V-1*		3W-C	2.0	C
23.07.44	F/O Gerard **Jongbloed**	RAF No. 104592	(NL)/RAF	*V-1*	RB171	3W-E	1.0	C
	F/O Coenraad **Manders**	RAF No. 113889	(NL)/RAF	*V-1*		3W-Y	1.0	C
24.07.44	F/O Rudolph **Burgwal**	RAF No. 113893	(NL)/RAF	*V-1*		3W-K	0.5	C
	F/O Jan **Jonker**	RAF No. 132082	(NL)/RAF			3W-D	0.5	C
26.07.44	F/O Jan van **Arkel**	RAF No. 124639	(NL)/RAF	*V-1*		3W-W	1.0	C
	F/Sgt Cornelis **Kooy**	RAF No. 1814967	(NL)/RAF	*V-1*		3W-S	1.0	C
	F/O Rudolph **Burgwal**	RAF No. 113893	(NL)/RAF	*V-1*	NH649	3W-F	1.0	C
	F/O Rudolph **Burgwal**	RAF No. 113893	(NL)/RAF	*V-1*	NH649	3W-F	0.5	C
	F/O Rudolph **Burgwal**	RAF No. 113893	(NL)/RAF	*V-1*	NH649	3W-F	0.5	C
28.07.44	F/Sgt Martinus **Janssen**	RAF No. 1814942	(NL)/RAF	*V-1*		3W-D	0.5	C
	Maj Keith C. **Kuhlmann**	SAAF No. P102441	SAAF	*V-1*	NH718	3W-G	1.0	C
29.07.44	F/O Mijnard van **Bergen**	RAF No. 113896	(NL)/RAF	*V-1*		3W-T	1.0	C
	F/O Lambert **Wolters**	RAF No. 141896	(NL)/RAF	*V-1*		3W-N	0.5	C
30.07.44	F/O Rudolph **Burgwal**	RAF No. 113893	(NL)/RAF	*V-1*		3W-C	1.0	C
02.08.44	F/Sgt Ronald van **Beers**	RAF No. 1814965	(NL)/RAF	*V-1*		3W-C	0.5	C
	F/Sgt Ronald van **Beers**	RAF No. 1814965	(NL)/RAF	*V-1*		3W-C	1.0	C
04.08.44	F/O Jan van **Arkel**	RAF No. 124639	(NL)/RAF	*V-1*		3W-W	1.0	C

Date	Pilot		S/N	Origin	Serial		Code		Fate
	F/L Jan **PLESMAN**	RAF No. 102524	(NL)/RAF	*V-1*			3W-Z	1.0	C
05.08.44	F/O Jan **JONKER**	RAF No. 132082	(NL)/RAF	*V-1*			3W-K	1.0	C
	F/O Rudolph **BURGWAL**	RAF No. 113893	(NL)/RAF	*V-1*	**RB184**		3W-B	2.0	C
06.08.44	F/L Jan **PLESMAN**	RAF No. 102524	(NL)/RAF	*V-1*			3W-P	1.0	C
07.08.44	F/O Rudolph **BURGWAL**	RAF No. 113893	(NL)/RAF	*V-1*			3W-L	1.0	C
09.08.44	F/L Leendert **VAN EENDENBURG**	RAF No. 108814	(NL)/RAF	*V-1*			3W-I	1.0	C
10.08.44	F/L Jan **PLESMAN**	RAF No. 102524	(NL)/RAF	*V-1*			3W-W	1.0	C

Total: 119.0 V-1s

The top Dutch V-1 scorer was F/O Rudy Burgwal. Born in the Dutch East Indies, he escaped from Holland in September 1941 and joined the RAF on arrival. Trained, he was then posted to 322 Sqn in July 1943. He was posted missing, shortly after the conversion to Spitfire IXs, on 12 August while escorting Lancasters.

Summary of the aircraft lost on Operations - 322 Squadron

Date	Pilot	S/N	Origin	Serial	Code	Fate
02.05.44	Sgt Henric **ROOVERS**	RAF No. 1814943	(NL)/RAF	**RB141**	VL-L	†
31.05.44	F/Sgt Cornelis **KOOY**	RAF No. 1814967	(NL)/RAF	**NH687**	VL-Q	-
12.07.44	W/O Justin **MAIER**	RAF No. 1549995	(NL)/RAF	**RM678**	3W-Q	†

Total: 3

Summary of the aircraft lost by accident - 322 Squadron

Date	Pilot	S/N	Origin	Serial	Code	Fate
11.04.44	F/O Jabob **VAN HAMEL**	RAF No. 132085	(NL)/RAF	**NH700**	VL-P	†

Total: 1

IN MEMORIAM

Spitfire Mk XIV - The Belgian and Dutch Squadrons

Name	Service No	Rank	Age	Origin	Date	Serial
GROENSTEEN, Jacques Alexandre H.P.	RAF No. 1299851	F/Sgt	22	(BEL)/RAF	20.04.45	NH686
HUENS, Robert Nicolas	RAF No. 1899804	F/Sgt	25	(BEL)/RAF	23.01.45	NH711
MAIER, Justin Albert	RAF No. 1549995	W/O	28	(NL)/RAF	12.07.44	RM678
MOREL, Mathieu Jean Joseph François	RAF No. 1424812	F/Sgt	22	(BEL)/RAF	11.11.44	RB168
ROOVERS, Henric Christian Anton	RAF No. 1814943	Sgt	25	(NL)/RAF	02.05.44	RB141
VANDERPERREN, Jacob Marie Francis	RAF No. 120896	F/O	24	(BEL)/RAF	25.12.44	RM673
VAN HAMEL, Jacob Willem	RAF No. 132085	F/O	23	(NL)/RAF	11.04.44	NH700

Total: 7

Belgium: 4, Netherlands: 3

Four Belgian pilots were killed while flying a Spitfire XIV in WW2:
Top left, F/Sgt 'Pichon' Groensteen who arrived in the UK in May 1940 as a refugee. He initially joined the Belgian Army before to be transferred to the RAF in August 1941. He served in both Belgian 349 and 350 Squadrons and it was his second tour of operations when he was killed. Bottom left, F/Sgt M. Morel. He left Belgium to join Great-Britain in 1941 and reached Gibraltar in July that year after having been interned for a little while in Spain. He had been posted to 350 in January 1944 for his first operational assignment. F/Sgt R. Huens (top right) was a pre-war military pilot and fought during the short May 1940 campaign. He was liberated and returned to Belgium; he eventually left the country in June 1942. His travel was far to be easy and reached Lisbon in Portugal in March 1943 from where he joined the UK soon after. Enlisting in the RAF on arrival he was posted to 350 in June 1944 upon his training completed. 'Butch' Vanderperen (bottom right) was a pre-war Belgian Army officer in the artillery. He escaped in August 1941 and joined Great Britain in December and enlisted in the RAF in February 1942. He had served with 349 before to be posted to 350 in June 1944.
(André Bar)

Supermarine Spitfire Mk.XIV RM693
No. 350 (Belgian) Squadron
Lympne (UK), August 1944

Supermarine Spitfire Mk.XIV NH689
No. 350 (Belgian) Squadron
Squadron Leader Terence SPENCER (RAF)
Y.32/Ophoven (Belgium), January 1945

Supermarine Spitfire Mk. XIV MV267
No. 350 (Belgian) Squadron
B.172/Husum (Germany), June–July 1945

Supermarine Spitfire Mk.XIV NH700
No. 322 (Dutch) Squadron
Acklington (UK), March 1944

Supermarine Spitfire Mk.XIV NH718
No. 322 (Dutch) Squadron
Major Keith C. KUHLMANN (SAAF)
West Malling (UK), June-July 1944

Supermarine Spitfire Mk.XIV NH699
No. 322 (Ducth) Squadron
Dealand (UK), August 1944

NB: No D-Day stripes were painted on this aircraft, profile made from a wartime footage

SQUADRONS! - The series

Donald James Matthew BLAKESLEE DFC

Supermarine Spitfire Mk.VB EN951
No. 133 (Eagle) Squadron
Flight Lieutenant D. J. M. Blakeslee
CAN./ J.4551
Gravesend (UK), August 1942

Charles Cuthbertson LEARMONTH DFC*

Douglas Boston Mk. III A28-9 (ex-AL691)
No. 22 Squadron RAAF
Squadron Leader C. C. Learmonth
A11.383
Port Moresby (New Guinea), spring 1943

Hans Anton MAURENBRECHER

Curtiss P-40N-35-CU C3-560
No. 120 (NEI) Squadron
Major H. Maurenbrecher
Biak (New Guinea), 1945-1946

Roland Prosper BEAMONT DSO* DFC*

Hawker Tempest Mk V JN751
No. 150 Wing
Wing Commander R. P. Beamont
RAF No. 41800
Bradwell Bay (UK), April 1944

Ronald Thomas SUSANS DSO DFC

North American P-51D-25-NT A68-724
No. 77 Squadron, RAAF
Squadron Leader R. T. Susans
G4392
Bofu (Japan), 1946

James Henry LACEY DFM*

Supermarine Spitfire Mk.XIV RN135
No. 17 Squadron
Squadron Leader J. H. Lacey
RAF No. 112709
Seletar (Singapore), autumn 1945

Introducing's RAF In Combat and Bravo Bravo Aviation's collection of highly-detailed and historically accurate, high-quality aviation prints.
For more information on available prints, please visit :

or

Keith Cowie KUHLMANN DFC

Supermarine Spitfire Mk.XIV NH718
No. 322 (Dutch) Squadron
Major K. C. Kuhlmann (SAAF)
SAAF No. P102441V
West Malling (UK), June-July 1944

Léopold COLLIGNON

RAF No. 116288

Supermarine Spitfire Mk.XIV RM693
No. 350 (Belgian) Squadron
Lympne (UK), autumn 1944

Prints available for this book:

PL-002: KC Kuhlmann
PL-062: T Spencer
PL-121: HE Walmsley
PL-126: L Collignon
PL-296: J Plesman